CW01430864

ZACK C. WOOTEN

Unauthorized Biography of J. R. R Tolkien

*From Philologist to Fantasy Maestro, Unveiling the Life
and Imagination of the Creator of Middle-earth*

Copyright © 2024 by Zack C. Wooten

All rights reserved. No part of this publication may be reproduced, stored or transmitted in any form or by any means, electronic, mechanical, photocopying, recording, scanning, or otherwise without written permission from the publisher. It is illegal to copy this book, post it to a website, or distribute it by any other means without permission.

Zack C. Wooten asserts the moral right to be identified as the author of this work.

First edition

This book was professionally typeset on Reedsy.
Find out more at reedsy.com

Contents

Chapter 1: Roots of John Reuel

Early Years in Bloemfontein

Full Name : John Ronald Reuel Tolkien
  Place of birth : Bloemfontein, an Afrikaans-speaking area of South Africa
  Date of Birth: 3 January 1892
  Date of death: 2 September 1973
  Occupation : English writer and philologist
  Nationality : British

Childhood in South Africa

J.R.R. Tolkien, the genius behind Middle-earth, came into the world on January 3, 1892, in the lively city of Bloemfontein, located in the heart of the Orange Free State, South Africa. His birth, a moment of quiet importance, marked the beginning of a life meant for creative greatness.

Tolkien's parents, **Arthur Reuel Tolkien** and **Mabel Suffield**, were English expats seeking a new life in the southern hemisphere. Arthur, a banker by profession, moved the family to South Africa in search of bright prospects. It was against this background of a growing country that John Ronald Reuel Tolkien, affectionately known as Ronald, started his trip.

The Tolkien home in Bloemfontein was a patchwork of family love. Mabel,

Ronald's mother, played a key part in his early upbringing. She instilled in him a love for stories and languages, setting the basis for the imaginary worlds that would later define his writing works.

Tragically, the Tolkiens' South African idyll was short-lived. When Ronald was just three years old, his father passed away suddenly. The loss of his father and the subsequent return to England left a lasting mark on young Ronald, forming the themes of loss and desire that would later dominate his stories.

Despite the difficulties, South Africa remained in Tolkien's mind as a place of important events. The scenery, the people, and the cultural variety left a mark on his artistic mind. The wealth of this early exposure to different cultures would later find expression in the colorful tapestry of Middle-earth.

In the simplicity of Bloemfontein's streets and the hug of family, J.R.R. Tolkien's childhood in South Africa sowed the seeds of a vast imagination. Little did he know that the echoes of these early years would resonate across time and space, making their way into the fabric of one of the most fascinating literary works ever written.

Early Influences on Tolkien's Imagination

J.R.R. Tolkien's trip into the worlds of fantasy was a symphony of diverse influences that played a unified tune throughout his early years. As the young Ronald submerged himself in the rich patchwork of life, various elements combined, feeding the seeds of creation that would bloom into the colorful settings of Middle-earth.

One deep impact was the wild world. Growing up in the rural settings of Sarehole and Birmingham, England, Tolkien found comfort and inspiration in the beauty of nature. The rolling hills, thick woods, and babbling brooks became the canvas upon which his imaginative images were painted. The beautiful scenery established in him a deep appreciation for the connection of all living things—a theme that would repeat in the intelligent landscapes of Middle-earth.

Language, too, became a powerful trigger for Tolkien's mind.

His interest with philology—the study of languages—began early. The mosaic of language variety interested him, and the finding of Finnish, Welsh, and Old English opened doors to old stories and myths. These linguistic excursions laid the basis for the creation of complex languages like Elvish in his imaginary world.

Tolkien's great desire for books further stoked the fire of his fantasy. He dove into old epics, Norse sagas, and the Arthurian tales, learning the details of storytelling and the rich cultural patchwork of bygone times. These literary gems became a source from which he drew inspiration, creating the story frameworks and magical aspects in his own works.

The art of speaking, imbibed from his mother Mabel, became a guiding light. Her tales of dragons, heroes, and far-off places became the first whispers of the epic sagas that would define Tolkien's literary heritage. Her influence not only encouraged a love for stories but also instilled in him the strong belief in the power of myth to convey greater truths.

Religion and the Catholic faith played a key part in Tolkien's upbringing.

The traditions, symbols, and moral lessons rooted in his faith added levels of complexity to his fantasy world. The theme of eucatastrophe—a sudden and happy turn of events—reflects Tolkien's religious viewpoint and is woven into the fabric of his stories.

Family and Tragedy

Impact of Parental Loss on Young Tolkien

J.R.R. Tolkien's early life was marked by the ebb and flow of family links, and yet, within this delicate weave, the thread of sadness worked its way through, leaving a permanent mark on the young Tolkien.

The loss of his father, Arthur Tolkien, when Ronald was but a young three years old, cast a long shadow over his youth. The rapid exit of the father, a figure of direction and security, threw the family into an emotional storm. The effect resonated through the Tolkien home, leaving young Ronald wrestling with the deep lack of father presence.

The lack of a father figure was strongly felt, and Tolkien's mother, Mabel, found herself managing the complicated difficulties of single parenting. In the face of hardship, Mabel became a symbol of resolve, teaching in her children a sense of courage and drive. However, the void left by Arthur's exit was a heartbreaking reminder of the fragility of family happiness.

The financial strains brought about by Arthur's passing forced the family to return to England. The move, while a realistic choice, marked a break from the sunny fields of South Africa and the dreams of a wealthy future. The comfort of familiar settings was replaced by the insecurity of a new beginning.

For young Ronald, the loss of his father became a source of mental depth. The themes of separation, longing, and the ache of family absence would later repeat in the complex relationships of his creative works. The poignant thread of desire, etched in the weave of Middle-earth, drew its inspiration from the emotional furnace of Tolkien's early years.

The effect of parental loss appeared not only in the emotional environment of Tolkien's mind but also in the subjects of his tales. Characters such as Frodo Baggins, Aragorn, and even Sauron represent the complex balance of power, loss, and the lasting quest for connection—a mirror of the author's own journey through the depths of grief.

In the furnace of family and disaster, J.R.R. Tolkien's perseverance and creation found a mutual relationship. The sounds of loss became a heartbreaking tune in the music of his stories, a testament to the changing power of personal experience on the canvas of literary creation.

Sibling Bonds and Family Dynamics

Within the limits of the Tolkien home, sibling bonds developed as strong threads creating a fabric of family connection. As young Ronald traveled the landscapes of his formative years, the dynamics of friendship and family relationships played a key role in forming his outlook and later, the themes of his creative works.

Ronald's bond with his younger brother, Hilary, became a cornerstone of his life. United by the common thread of shared experiences and family difficulties, the Tolkien brothers formed a friendship that would weather the storms of life. The friendship offered a source of strength, a shared haven in the face of the void left by their father's sudden exit.

The dynamics of family bonds brightened the Tolkien home with moments of laughter, shared secrets, and the silent understanding that often marks the relationships between brothers. Hilary, a steady partner in the trip through childhood, became not only a buddy but a confidant—a co-conspirator in the fantasy worlds that Ronald began to build.

Family relations, supported by the strong presence of their mother, Mabel, brought a sense of togetherness amid the difficulties they faced. Mabel's resilience and drive in the wake of widowhood set the tone for the family's joint journey. Her role as both nurturer and giver stressed the value of family ties as a source of support and security.

The balance of family dynamics, with its joys and difficulties, found expression in the characters and relationships within Tolkien's creative works. Frodo and Sam's unshakable friendship, the complex dynamics among the members of the Fellowship, and the family echoes in the House of Elrond all show signs of the familial fabric that shaped the author's outlook.

As Tolkien managed the complex dance of brother bonds and family relationships, he drew from the wellsprings of his own experiences to infuse sincerity into his writing. The details of friendship, the shared loads of hardship, and the unbreakable bonds that bind brothers became thematic pillars in the building of Middle-earth—a testament to the lasting effect of family relationships on the weave of J.R.R. Tolkien's life and literary legacy.

Chapter 2: Scholarly Pursuits

Oxford Years

Academic Pursuits at Exeter College

J.R.R. Tolkien's stay at Oxford marked a changing chapter in his life—a period of intellectual growth, deep bonds, and the completion of his academic interests. As he stepped onto the ancient grounds of Exeter College, the sounds of Sarehole and Birmingham gradually gave way to the hallowed halls of academics.

The academic tapestry at Exeter College, where Tolkien continued his college studies, offered a rich environment for the growing scholar. The study of a classics degree became the furnace in which his language and literary emotions found an organized and academic expression. The lively intellectual atmosphere, filled with arguments, talks, and the search of knowledge, sparked the fires of Tolkien's academic interest.

It was within the confines of Exeter College that Tolkien's fascination with philology—the study of language in history texts—flourished. The complexities of Old English, Old Norse, and Gothic languages became not just subjects of study but entrances to the rich fabric of old tales and sagas.
The linguistic playground at Exeter laid the basis for Tolkien's future projects, particularly the creation of the complex languages that would

breathe life into the societies of Middle-earth.

Beyond the classroom rooms, the friendship of like-minded students created the Inklings—a literary study group that included stars such as C.S. Lewis and Owen Barfield. This company of minds became a furnace for the exchange of ideas, reviews, and the nurturing of creative sparks. The intellectual activity of the Inklings was important in forming Tolkien's thoughts on myth, stories, and the deep effect of language on culture.

Yet, the Oxford years were not without their difficulties. The threat of World War I cast its shadow, and many of Tolkien's peers, including close friends, joined in the war. The war, a furnace of loss and sacrifice, would later infuse Tolkien's works with themes of courage, friendship, and the cost of great acts.

As Tolkien engaged himself in the academic life of Exeter College, the roots were made for the rise of a creative giant. The fusion of academic seriousness, language passion, and the furnace of military events would combine into the literary magic that created works like "The Hobbit" and "The Lord of the Rings." The Oxford years were not merely a time of academic study; they were the forge in which the great tales of Middle-earth began to take shape, expecting their moment to enchant the world.

Formation of the T.C.B.S. (Tea Club, Barrovian Society)

Within the ancient walls of King Edward's School in Birmingham, an association was formed that would overcome the limits of academics and spark the creative souls of its members. The origin of the T.C.B.S.—the Tea Club, Barrovian Society—marked a key moment in J.R.R. Tolkien's life, combining friendship, intellectual interests, and the forming of ties that would survive the tests of time.

The T.C.B.S. came from the friendship of four like-minded souls: J.R.R.

Tolkien, Geoffrey Bache Smith, Christopher Wiseman, and Robert Gilson. United by a shared love for literature, a sense of friendship, and a vision for artistic and literary efforts, these young men formed a family that would play a crucial role in forming Tolkien's literary journey.

The meetings of the T.C.B.S. were not mere parties but crucibles of creation, intellectual discovery, and the sharing of dreams. The group's name, a playful mix of friendship and a nod to the Barrow Stores where they gathered, captured the spirit of their fellowship—a meeting that transcended formalities and welcomed the warmth of shared interests.

As the members of the T.C.B.S. managed the move from school to university life, their bond strengthened. Discussions on books, language, and the artistic projects they envisioned became the heart of their relationship. Tolkien, in particular, found in the T.C.B.S. a welcoming group that fostered his growing writing dreams.

The start of World War I put a cloud over the T.C.B.S. as its members joined in the service, with some giving the final price. The loss of Robert Gilson, a dear friend and a founding member, was a deep blow that rippled through Tolkien's life and repeated in the themes of loss and sacrifice woven into his later works.

The impact of the T.C.B.S., however, continued beyond the war. Tolkien, greatly affected by the war and the loss of his friends, took the spirit of the company into his writing efforts. The themes of camaraderie, the forming of unexpected partnerships, and the lasting power of friendship became basic elements in the tales of Middle-earth.

The formation of the T.C.B.S. was more than a young meeting; it was a furnace that shaped J.R.R. Tolkien's artistic spirit. The memories of their unity, talks, and shared dreams stayed in the hallways of his mind, filling his works with the timeless magic of lasting friendship.

Language and Mythology

Tolkien's Love for Linguistics

At the heart of J.R.R. Tolkien's creative talent lay a deep love for language—a passion that surpassed the limits of education and became a cornerstone in the building of Middle-earth. As a philologist, Tolkien's language interests not only shaped his academic endeavors but also became the rich soil from which his magical tales would spring forth.

Tolkien's linguistic journey started with the love for the details of words, the origin of languages, and the beauty of syntactic structures. This interest, sparked in his early years, bloomed during his academic activities at Oxford, where he dove into the study of Old English, Old Norse, and Gothic languages. These old tongues, with their rich histories and cultural nuances, became the first strokes on the painting of his language love.

One of Tolkien's most amazing linguistic creations was the Elvish language. Far beyond the needs of stories, he carefully created not one, but multiple Elvish languages—Quenya and Sindarin—each with its own grammar, structure, and vocabulary. The languages were not simply a background for his tales but live, breathing beings with a depth that reflected the complexity of real-world languages.

The process of language creation for Tolkien was not random. The sounds, the beat, and the cultural background of each imagined language were carefully studied. In his search of linguistic realism, Tolkien tried to create languages that felt organic, languages that carried the weight of history and culture within their sound details.

The deep relationship between language and mythology became obvious as Tolkien filled his linguistic works with the tales and stories of Middle-earth. The languages were not separate things but carriers that carried the cultural traditions, tales, and memories of the peoples who spoke them. This blend of language and story created a unique narrative style that set Tolkien's works apart in the world of fantasy fiction.

The Silmarillion, Tolkien's mythopoeic work, demonstrates the smooth merging of language and magical aspects. The creation myth, the histories of the Elves, and the great tales were sewn into the linguistic fabric of Middle-earth, creating a unified and engaging world where language was not a mere tool but an important part of the storytelling.

Tolkien's love for linguistics, showing in the creation of complex languages and the study of historical depths, became a defining feature of his literary heritage. The fusion of linguistic talent and mythopoeic stories in Middle-earth stands as a testament to the deep effect that a scholar's love for language can have on the worlds of fantasy.

Early works and how the Elvish languages came to be

When J.R.R. Tolkien first started to be creative, he used language invention and mythological stories together in a way that worked well. As he started to write his legendarium, the first seeds of Middle-earth were planted. At the same time, he carefully worked on languages, especially the Elvish languages of Quenya and Sindarin.

Tolkien's journey with language started long before he thought of the stories that would take place in Middle-earth. He first tried coming up with new words because he wanted to make up a story for England. This project grew into The Silmarillion, a huge work of literature.

Tolkien's poems and writing from the early 1910s were the first to show signs of Elvish languages. "The Shores of Faëry" and "The Happy Mariners" were early poems that had sounds that would later become part of Quenya.

11

These bits and pieces of language were basically the early stages of the Elvish languages that would eventually take over Middle-earth's language environment.

In 1918, stories and songs written in the lines of World War I were put together in "The Book of Lost Tales," which became a big deal. Tolkien wrote the first drafts of the legendarium that would become The Silmarillion in these stories. This time saw the birth of the High Elvish language, Quenya, as well as the creation of the deep, musical tongue of the Grey-elves, Sindarin.

Tolkien's language creation was not a distant academic exercise but a spontaneous extension of his stories. The Elvish languages were imagined as live beings, complete with grammatical rules, vocabulary, and a historical growth that matched the creation of real-world languages.

The linguistic environment of Middle-earth grew further with "The Lays of Beleriand" and the growth of the Elvish languages continued in line with the development of The Silmarillion. Quenya, the language of the High Elves, became the vehicle for the polished, courtly expression of Elvish culture, while Sindarin, the tongue of the Grey-elves, carried a more casual and musical rhythm.

Tolkien's commitment to language accuracy was unmatched. His creation of the Elvish languages went beyond the needs of stories, becoming an engaging experience for readers. The linguistic depth, complexity, and cultural impact of the Elvish languages added levels of credibility to the mythic weave of Middle-earth, setting a standard for linguistic creation in the realm of fantasy fiction.

Chapter 3: War and Creation

World War I

Tolkien's Experience on the Western Front

World War I, often referred to as Great War, changed the course of history and left a lasting mark on those who lived through its terrible circumstances. J.R.R. Tolkien, famous for his literary contributions to fiction, underwent a changing trip on the Western Front—one that would deeply affect both his personal outlook and the thematic elements woven into the fabric of Middle-earth.

The war began in 1914, drawing in millions of young men like Tolkien into the chaos of combat. As a young soldier in the British Army, Tolkien's trip into the ditches of the Western Front became a furnace that tried his grit, formed lasting bonds, and etched the grim facts of battle into the depths of his mind.

Mobilization and the Somme Campaign

In 1915, Tolkien enrolled in the Lancashire Fusiliers, and by the following year, he found himself on the Western Front. The Battle of the Somme, one of the most dreaded and deadly fights of the war, became a defining moment in Tolkien's military service. The sights and sounds of the battlefield, the unity amidst the chaos, and the ever-present threat of death left a lasting imprint on his mind.

Tolkien's experiences during the Somme Campaign were hard and at times terrible. The trench combat, marked by mud-soaked landscapes and constant shooting, was a terrifying scene that tried the resolve of those who experienced it. The painful facts of warfare penetrated Tolkien's mind, finding expression in the sad landscapes and battlescapes of Middle-earth.

Fellowship and Loss

In the crucible of war, Tolkien made deep and lasting bonds with fellow fighters. The friendship formed amidst the horrors of the ditches became a source of comfort and strength. The T.C.B.S., or Tea Club, Barrovian Society, a company of Tolkien and his closest friends, was permanently changed by the war. Rob Gilson, a beloved member of the group, fell in the Battle of the Somme, a loss that ran through Tolkien's life and later repeated in the themes of friendship and suffering within his literary works.

The T.C.B.S. had been a furnace of inspiration, a place for shared ideas and ambitions. The war, however, left its long cloud, scattering the company as its members went off to fight. The loss of Gilson marked the first of many wartime deaths that would shape Tolkien's outlook and affect the tales of Middle-earth.

Creativity in the Midst of Chaos

Amidst the chaos of war, Tolkien's artistic spirit survived. It was during his time on the Western Front that he started laying the roots for what would later become The Silmarillion and The Lord of the Rings. The imaginative settings of Middle-earth served as a haven from the hard realities of the ditches, providing Tolkien with a mental sanctuary where he could escape during times of relief.

The creation of languages, especially the Elvish tongues of Quenya and Sindarin, became a linguistic practice that merged with Tolkien's battle experiences. The gloomy rhythm of Elvish languages reflected the sad tones of the war-ravaged landscapes, giving a poignant outlet for Tolkien's feelings and thoughts.

The Impact of War on Tolkien's Mythopoeia

The war, with its bloodshed and loss, deeply shaped Tolkien's mythopoeic vision. The theme of eucatastrophe, a sudden and joyful turn of events, came as a reaction to the bleakness of war. In the face of crushing darkness, Tolkien's tales welcomed the possibility of unexpected hope and redemption—an echo of his own survival against the odds.

The Scouring of the Shire, a final event in The Lord of the Rings, draws comparisons to the destruction caused by war. The marks of fighting, the relocation of communities, and the sad return to familiar settings reflected the post-war realities that Tolkien and many others faced.

Reflections on Power and Corruption

Tolkien's views of power dynamics and the evil effect of total power found expression in the character of Sauron. The Dark Lord's relentless quest for control over Middle-earth matched the authoritarian beliefs that drove the war. The One Ring, a sign of total power, became a story device through which Tolkien explored the moral difficulties of exercising unlimited authority.

The industrialization of battle, experienced by Tolkien during the war, affected the picture of Saruman's war machine in Isengard. The despoiling of nature, the mass production of weapons, and the disregard for the sanctity of life echoed the horrors of the mechanical fighting that marked World War I.

Legacy of War in Middle-earth

The war's impact affects Middle-earth, forming the moral environment and thematic roots of Tolkien's works. The battles against crushing odds, the ties of friendship that survive through hardship, and the healing power of small acts of heroism—all find echoes in the tales that played on the Western

Front.

The Dead Marshes, an eerie setting in The Lord of the Rings, takes inspiration from Tolkien's memories of the war. The ghost of fallen troops, the weight of their unmet hopes, and the otherworldly quality of the swamps refer to the deep effect of war on the human mind.

The concept of Mordor, a land scarred by the insidious impact of evil, mirrors the post-war despair and the knowledge of the harmful potential within humanity. The war's fallout, with its global changes and social shifts, found meaning in Tolkien's picture of Middle-earth as a world dealing with the memories of past wars.

Writing Amidst the Horrors of War: Tolkien's Literary Alchemy

The furnace of war, with its horrors and hardships, became an odd source for the creative magic of J.R.R. Tolkien. As the Great War went on, Tolkien, an officer on the Western Front, found comfort and inspiration in the act of writing. The combination of imagination and chaos birthed the foundations of Middle-earth, setting the groundwork for tales that would fascinate generations.

A Haven in Imagination

The ditches of the Western Front were a sharp contrast to the worlds of fiction that Tolkien would later build. Amidst the mud, the constant shooting, and the overwhelming threat of death, Tolkien found shelter in the imagined settings of his own creation. The act of world-building became a mental refuge, a place where he could briefly flee the grim facts of war.

In the quiet times between fights, Tolkien would escape into the folds of his thoughts, where the landscapes of Middle-earth spread like a vast fabric. The green fields of the Shire, the ancient trees of Lothlórien, and the tall peaks of the Misty Mountains became not just escape dreams but healing settings that soothed the scars of war.

Linguistic Pursuits in the Trenches

Tolkien's linguistic interests, especially the creation of Elvish languages, thrived amidst the chaos of war. The careful creation of languages such as Quenya and Sindarin became a form of linguistic escape. In the quiet times of relief, Tolkien would dig into the details of phonetics, spelling, and words, forming the linguistic roots of Middle-earth.

The Elvish languages, born in the battles, were not mere constructs for stories but live, breathing beings that carried the weight of Tolkien's feelings and thoughts. The rhythmic cadences of Elvish became a balm for the chaos of war, a linguistic beauty that chimed with the author's deep love for language.

The Birth of The Silmarillion

It was during the war that Tolkien started sketching the early versions of what would later become The Silmarillion. The tales of the Elder Days, the origin story, and the deaths of Elves and Men played in the margins of his military-issued notes. The act of retelling, often done under the dim light of a trench lamp, became a link to a world untouched by the horrors of war.

The Silmarillion, in its initial form, acted as a testament to Tolkien's resolve in the face of hardship. The tales, though scattered and disjointed, bore the seeds of the rich mythopoeia that would later enchant readers worldwide. The war, with its widespread sense of loss, became a thematic furnace that shaped the tone and story arcs within The Silmarillion.

Camaraderie and Storytelling

In the company of fellow soldiers, Tolkien found an audience for his growing stories. Around campfires and in the lulls between battles, he would regale his friends with stories from the rich fabric of Middle-earth. The act of storytelling became a community experience, a shared trip into places far away from the horrors of the Western Front.

The T.C.B.S., despite the difficulties of military separation, continued to play a role in Tolkien's artistic efforts. Letters shared between friends held bits of tales, language thoughts, and comments on the effect of war. The company, though physically scattered, stayed joined through the imagined lines spun by Tolkien's stories.

Loss and the Redemptive Power of Art

The war exacted a toll on Tolkien's personal life, marked by the loss of close friends and the troubling memories of the battlefield. The death of Rob Gilson, a beloved member of the T.C.B.S., was a deep blow that repeated in Tolkien's literary works. The theme of selfless friendship, obvious in the bond between Frodo and Sam, reflected the lasting effect of wartime loss on the author's mind.

Art, for Tolkien, became a healing force—a means of making sense of the meaningless, of finding beauty amidst the violence. The act of creation, whether through words or stories, became a form of defiance against the demeaning effects of war. The Silmarillion, though not finished during Tolkien's lifetime, stood as a testament to the changing power of art in the face of crushing darkness.

The Influence of War on Middle-earth

The war's impact on Tolkien's work went beyond the thematic details to the very structure of Middle-earth. The bleak regions of Mordor, scarred by the machines of war, mirrored the manufactured destruction viewed by Tolkien on the Western Front. The Dead Marshes, spooky and ghostly, drew inspiration from the eerie landscapes of no man's land, cursed by the fallen.

The battles of Frodo and his friends against impossible odds reflected the resiliency of the human spirit in the face of war's horrors. The idea of eucatastrophe, a sudden and happy turn of events, came as a reaction to the widespread bleakness of war—a storytelling device that carried echoes of hope amidst sadness.

Creation of Middle-earth

Birth of Hobbits and the World of The Silmarillion

In the vast fabric of J.R.R. Tolkien's mind, the creation of Middle-earth emerged as a grand work, sewing together complex tales, lively cultures, and diverse races. At the heart of this magical realm lay the birth of Hobbits and the basic tales told in The Silmarillion.

The origin of Middle-earth, marked by language creation and mythopoeic brilliance, produced a world that would capture the minds of readers for generations.

Linguistic Alchemy

Tolkien's trip into Middle-earth began with his love for languages. The development of Elvish languages, Quenya and Sindarin, came not as a mere linguistic exercise but as an important factor in the world-building process. The sound subtleties, linguistic structures, and historical roots of these languages became the base upon which Middle-earth would grow.

The Elvish languages were not separate products; they were linked with the stories and cultures of the races that spoke them. The accuracy and sincerity with which Tolkien created these languages added a layer of depth to Middle-earth, creating a linguistic setting that reflected the complexities of the real world.

The Silmarillion

As Tolkien dove into the creation of languages, the tales of The Silmarillion began to take shape. This important book, often referred to as Tolkien's "Legendarium," recounts the fictional history of Middle-earth, from the birth of the world to the end of the Third Age. The Silmarillion is a tale of sorrow, courage, and the timeless battle between light and evil.

The Ainulindalë, the creation story within The Silmarillion, opens as a chorus of heavenly beings, the Ainur, sharing in the making of the world. The reverberation of this mythic creation story reverberates throughout the following tales, affecting the fate of Elves, Men, Dwarves, and the very land of Middle-earth.

The Hobbits

While The Silmarillion laid the roots of Middle-earth's fictional past, the rise of Hobbits added a charming and surprising element to the tale. Hobbits, with their love for simple joys, farming activities, and a deep-seated dislike to journeys, became the key figures in Tolkien's later works, especially The Hobbit and The Lord of the Rings.

The Hobbits' birth was an exercise in parody of epic tropes. In a world ruled by great quests and epic battles, Tolkien presented a race of beings who found joy in the safety of home, the company of friends, and the farming of the earth. The Shire, the peaceful country of the Hobbits, became a miniature of rural happiness in the middle of a bigger, chaotic world.

Hobbits and The Lord of the Rings

The Hobbits took center stage in The Lord of the Rings, a massive work that built upon the story set in The Silmarillion. Frodo Baggins, Samwise Gamgee, and their friends went on a trip that would decide the fate of Middle-earth. The humble Hobbits, thrust into the furnace of world-altering events, emerged as unexpected heroes whose perseverance and friendship stood as a counterpoint to the darkness that threatened to engulf the land.

The creation of Hobbits highlighted Tolkien's ability to fill his world with diverse and familiar characters. Their journey, filled with challenges and moral complexities, became a testament to the lasting power of the individual in the face of crushing odds. The Shire, originally a haven of simplicity, changed into a sign of struggle against the growing shadows of Mordor.

Interconnected Narratives

The greatness of Tolkien's world-building lies in the interdependence of its tales. The Silmarillion, with its cosmic scale, laid the groundwork for the events that occurred in The Hobbit and The Lord of the Rings. Each tale, whether vast or personal, added to the rich weave of Middle-earth, producing a sense of continuity and depth that transcends the limits of traditional storytelling.

The Elves, with their sad past and lasting knowledge, played important parts in both The Silmarillion and The Lord of the Rings. The Dwarves, with their proud history and thirst for wealth, added to the complex web of alliances and battles. Men, the race of death, stood at the heart of both big sagas, wrestling with fate, courage, and the unavoidable passage of time.

Beginnings of The Hobbit and Its Impact

J.R.R. Tolkien's journey into Middle-earth continued with the humorous and surprising adventure of The Hobbit. The creation of this enchanting tale began as a bedtime story for Tolkien's children and grew into a literary gem that not only introduced readers to the world of Hobbits but also laid the foundation for the epic storylines that would follow. The Hobbit's effect goes far beyond its initial release, changing the course of fantasy fiction and solidifying Tolkien's reputation as a master writer.

The Origins of Bilbo's Journey

The origins of The Hobbit can be traced back to a simple yet deep starting. In the early 1930s, Tolkien, a father of four, started on the job of creating a bedtime story for his children. Little did he know that this tale, born out of love and family affection, would grow into a literary success that crossed age and time.

The protagonist of this tale was Bilbo Baggins, a modest Hobbit with a penchant for comfort and routine. Bilbo's trip, which initially began as a playful and funny adventure, soon took surprising turns as he found himself involved in the quest for wealth guarded by the fearsome dragon, Smaug. The Hobbit's early chapters, filled with Hobbit ideas and the charming quirks of Bilbo, set the stage for a tale that would connect with readers of all ages.

Literary Alchemy

The Hobbit, although initially meant for a younger audience, quickly caught the minds of readers beyond the world of children's fiction. Tolkien's superb use of language, his skilled mixing of humor and depth, and the creation of a compelling world marked by dwarves, elves, goblins, and, of course, the One Ring, raised The Hobbit into the realm of timeless classics.

The novel's effect lies not just in its storytelling brilliance but in its ability to evoke a sense of wonder and adventure. Bilbo's trip from the comfort of the Shire to the dangerous Lonely Mountain became a metaphor for the changing power of moving out of one's comfort zone. The themes of courage, friendship, and the surprising heroism of the most modest characters connected with a wide audience, overcoming the limits of age and genre.

The Ring and the Shaping of Middle-earth

The Hobbit, although written as a solo story, presented a powerful item that would play a key part in the larger legendarium—the One Ring. The benign golden ring, originally a mere trinket in Gollum's cave, became a harbinger of darkness and a key in the grand fabric of Middle-earth.

Tolkien's ability to predict the events of The Lord of the Rings within the pages of The Hobbit added a layer of complexity to the story. The slight links between Bilbo's adventure and the rising shadows of Mordor displayed Tolkien's skill in creating a unified and interconnected world.

Impact on Fantasy Literature

Published in 1937, The Hobbit left an enduring mark on the world of fantasy fiction. Its success not only made the way for Tolkien's following works but also inspired generations of writers who followed. The Hobbit's influence can be seen in the rise of a separate subgenre—epic fantasy—that loves rich world-building, complicated characters, and plots that transcend the everyday.

Tolkien's approach to writing, marked by language creativity, deep knowledge, and a strong understanding of ancient themes, became a pattern for hopeful fantasy writers. The Hobbit's ongoing success meant that Middle-earth would become a reference for readers wanting deep and broad imaginary worlds.

Adaptations and Continued Popularity

The Hobbit's impact stretches beyond the written page, finding new life in different versions. From cartoon pictures to the big movie series directed by Peter Jackson, Bilbo's trip has been brought to life on screens of all kinds. These versions, while meeting scrutiny for artistic freedoms, have presented Tolkien's world to audiences worldwide, promoting a fresh interest in Middle-earth.

The lasting success of The Hobbit is obvious in its continued influence in popular culture. From mentions in other works of literature to the marking of Hobbit Day on September 22nd, the impact of this humble tale stretches far and wide.

The Unassuming Epic

The Hobbit stands as a witness to the changing power of stories. What began as a bedtime story for Tolkien's children grew into a literary gem that spanned fields and generations. The effect of The Hobbit is not merely confined to the world of fantasy literature but stretches to the very core of storytelling—a warning that even the most modest of tales can start on trips that echo across time and space. Bilbo's journey, with its humor, heart, and courage, continues to invite readers to step into the enchanting world of Middle-earth, marking The Hobbit as a lasting classic in the list of literary gems.

Chapter 4: The Hobbit and The Lord of the Rings

The Hobbit: Unexpected Success

Writing Process and Publication Journey

The creation and release of J.R.R. Tolkien's "The Hobbit" was a trip marked by surprising turns, a charming protagonist, and the birth of a literary success. This chapter goes into the writing process of "The Hobbit" and explores its release journey, showing the chance and creative brilliance that resulted in the surprising success of this timeless classic.

The Genesis of Bilbo's Tale

"The Hobbit" began as a story told by Tolkien to entertain his children. The tale of Bilbo Baggins, a Hobbit who reluctantly goes on a big journey, was initially imagined during Tolkien's stay at the University of Oxford in the early 1930s. Inspired by his love for folklore and mythology, Tolkien wove a story that mixed traditional fairy-tale elements with the growing wealth of Middle-earth.

The writing process of "The Hobbit" was marked by freedom and a sense of discovery. Tolkien himself stated that he often did not know what would happen next in the story, leaving the plot to flow naturally. This method added to the playful and uncertain nature of Bilbo's trip, catching the spirit of a classic fairy story.

From Typescript to Publication

"The Hobbit" might have stayed a beloved family story if not for a stroke of chance. In the early 1930s, a typescript of the unfinished draft found its way to Susan Dagnall, a friend of Tolkien's who worked at the publishing company George Allen & Unwin. Intrigued by the tale, Dagnall shared it with Stanley Unwin, the firm's founder.

Unwin's ten-year-old son, Rayner, played a key part in the release choice. Tasked with reading the text, Rayner offered an enthusiastic recommendation, stating, "This is the best book I have ever read." Encouraged by Rayner's support, Unwin chose to print "The Hobbit."

In 1937, "The Hobbit" was publicly released to the public. The first version, having drawings by Tolkien himself, introduced readers to the fascinating world of Hobbits, dwarves, elves, and dragons. The initial print run of 1,500 copies sold out quickly, signaling the unexpected success that awaited Tolkien's tale.

Critical Acclaim and Popular Reception

"The Hobbit" earned critical praise for its storytelling charm, inventive world-building, and Tolkien's ability to capture the spirit of traditional tales. Readers of all ages were fascinated by Bilbo's trip, the questions with Gollum, the meeting with Smaug the dragon, and the Battle of the Five Armies. The novel's success stretched beyond the world of children's writing, finding a place among adult readers and experts.

The surprise success of "The Hobbit" led George Allen & Unwin to request a sequel. This request set the basis for what would later become "The Lord of the Rings" series. The Hobbit's effect on literature and popular culture was deep, affecting the course of fantasy fiction and solidifying Tolkien's status as a master writer.

The surprising success of "The Hobbit" is a testament to the global draw of stories that crosses age and genre. Tolkien's ability to craft a story that connects with the kid within each reader, combined with the magic of Middle-earth, guaranteed that Bilbo's tale would continue to be loved by generations to come.

Shaping the Foundations of Middle-earth

J.R.R. Tolkien's creative process in forming the foundations of Middle-earth was a massive task that involved language invention, mythopoeic vision, and a careful attention to detail. This chapter explores the complex weave of Middle-earth's creation, diving into Tolkien's language interests, the building of myths, and the basic elements that laid the base for the vast legendarium.

The Birth of Elvish Languages

Tolkien's trip into Middle-earth was separate from his love for languages. The creation of Elvish languages, such as Quenya and Sindarin, marked the origin of Middle-earth's linguistic setting. Tolkien, a philologist by study, dove into the details of sound, structure, and meaning, creating languages that were not mere constructs but live beings within the story.

The Elvish languages were more than a verbal experiment; they became the cultural and political base of the Elves, shaping the way they thought, expressed themselves, and viewed the world. The wealth of Elvish languages added to the realism and depth of Middle-earth, moving it beyond a mere background to a fully realized world with its own linguistic diversity.

The Creation of The Silmarillion

Tolkien's vision for Middle-earth went beyond language creativity to the making of myths. "The Silmarillion," a collection of linked epic tales, acted as the core book for Middle-earth's past. The Ainulindalë, the creation story within The Silmarillion, portrayed the making of the world by divine beings known as the Ainur, echoing Tolkien's belief in sub-creation as an act of mirroring the divine creation.

The Silmarillion wove tales of sad heroes, the battles between light and darkness, and the ebb and flow of societies. These myths, inspired by real-world mythologies and Tolkien's Catholic faith, added depth and meaning to Middle-earth, elevating it from a mere setting to a place filled with timeless themes and moral complexities.

Expanding the Narrative Horizon

While The Silmarillion built the magical roots, it was The Hobbit and The Lord of the Rings that brought Middle-earth to a greater audience. The Hobbit, initially a children's tale, exposed readers to the charming world of Hobbits, Dwarves, and dragons. The surprising success of The Hobbit led Tolkien to grow his legendarium, leading to the creation of The Lord of the Rings.

The Lord of the Rings, a massive tale, looked into the subtleties of power, friendship, and the inevitable passing of time. It drew on the magical lines set in The Silmarillion, weaving them into a story that covered countries and ages. The careful mix of people, languages, and cultures displayed Tolkien's commitment to a unified and linked world.

The Lord of the Rings: Epic Journey

Crafting the Trilogy

J.R.R. Tolkien's greatest work, "The Lord of the Rings," stands as an unmatched success in the realm of fantasy writing. This chapter dives into the epic journey of crafting the trilogy, studying Tolkien's creative process, the thematic depth of the narrative, and the lasting effect of Frodo's quest to destroy the One Ring.

The Creative Odyssey: From Hobbiton to Mordor

Tolkien's journey into "The Lord of the Rings" began as an unexpected sequel to the lighthearted adventure of "The Hobbit." The trip developed naturally as Tolkien managed the difficulties of Middle-earth's changing story. Initially intended as a single volume, the story grew into a multi-faceted tale that covered three books: "The Fellowship of the Ring," "The Two Towers," and "The Return of the King."

The making of "The Lord of the Rings" was marked by careful world-building, literary accuracy, and a dedication to consistency. Tolkien's deep knowledge of Middle-earth's past, cultures, and languages added to a tale that felt engaging and lived-in. The creative journey took Tolkien from the peaceful settings of the Shire to the heart of the dark realm of Mordor, building a tale of epic proportions.

Themes and Motifs: The Heart of the Ring

At the core of "The Lord of the Rings" lies a patchwork of themes and patterns that raise the story beyond a simple quest. The pervasive theme of power and its destructive effect, represented by the One Ring, serves as a moving force that changes the fates of individuals and countries. Friendship, suffering, and the endurance of the human spirit appear as repeated themes, connecting with readers on a deep level.

The idea of the hero's journey takes center stage as Frodo Baggins, followed by the Fellowship, goes on a dangerous quest to Mount Doom. The plot ties together multiple stories, from the wars of Gondor to the trials of Samwise Gamgee and Frodo's internal struggle against the draw of the Ring. The thematic depth of "The Lord of the Rings" ensures that it surpasses the limits of a traditional fantasy story, diving into universal truths and timeless human experiences.

The Fellowship: Characters and Relationships

"The Lord of the Rings" presents readers to a diverse array of people, each adding to the story in unique ways. From the sturdy Aragorn to the wise Gandalf, and the resilient Samwise to the troubled Gollum, the Fellowship represents a range of virtues and flaws. Tolkien's drive to building complex characters promotes a deep emotional link between readers and the residents of Middle-earth.

Central to the story is the lasting bond between Frodo and Sam, a connection that becomes the emotional center of the series. The dedication, sacrifice, and unshakable support between these two characters add a human layer to the story, grounding the magical tale in familiar feelings.

Linguistic Brilliance: Khuzdul, Quenya, and the Song of Durin

Tolkien's linguistic skill, showcased in the creation of languages like Khuzdul (Dwarvish) and Quenya (High Elvish), adds a layer of realism to the societies of Middle-earth. The Dwarven marks, Elvish markings, and the Song of Durin add to the engaging quality of the trilogy, allowing readers to connect with the language variety of Tolkien's world.

The addition of poems and songs, such as the Lament for Boromir and the Song of Durin, serves not only as a language showcase but also as a means of communicating the deep feelings and cultural memories of the characters. The language brilliance of "The Lord of the Rings" is not a mere accessory but an essential part of the story weave.

Translating Middle-earth to the Screen

The great trip of "The Lord of the Rings" stretched beyond the written page to the world of film. Directed by Peter Jackson, the film versions brought Middle-earth to life on the big screen. While adaptations often face challenges in catching the spirit of a literary work, Jackson's series earned broad praise for its faithfulness to the source material, visual show, and engaging performances.

The success of the film versions brought "The Lord of the Rings" to a global audience, sparking fresh interest in Tolkien's work and establishing Middle-earth as a movie landmark. The trilogy's influence on the fantasy genre in film cannot be stressed, setting a bar for world-building, visual effects, and plot.

Frodo's Final Steps

"The Lord of the Rings" ended with Frodo's final steps into the fiery pit of Mount Doom, where the One Ring was destroyed. The story came full circle as the characters faced the results of their decisions, and Middle-earth moved into a new age. The trilogy's impact is etched on the scenery of fantasy literature, inspiring later generations of authors to start on their creative odysseys.

Themes, Characters, and the Quest for the One Ring

"The Lord of the Rings" is a literary work that ties together complex themes, memorable characters, and a massive journey focused around the One Ring. In this chapter, we study the thematic depth, character interactions, and the overall goal that define the story and add to the lasting effect of J.R.R. Tolkien's epic trilogy.

Themes: Power, Friendship, and Sacrifice

At the heart of "The Lord of the Rings" are deep and timeless ideas that connect with viewers across generations. The theme of power and its evil effect is represented by the One Ring. From the seductive appeal it places on individuals to the harmful potential it possesses, the Ring becomes a sign of the moral difficulties surrounding the chase of power.

Friendship appears as a key theme, symbolized by the unity formed among people from various races and backgrounds. The ties between Frodo, Sam, Aragorn, Legolas, Gimli, Gandalf, and others demonstrate loyalty, friendship, and the power gained from unity. The theme of sacrifice runs through the story, as characters make selfless decisions for the greater good, epitomized by Frodo's burden to destroy the Ring at great personal cost.

Characters: Multidimensional Portrayals

"The Lord of the Rings" presents readers to a rich mix of people, each adding to the story in unique and important ways. Frodo Baggins, the humble Hobbit thrust into the role of the Ring-bearer, represents resolve, courage, and the responsibility of holding a world-altering treasure. His loyal partner, Samwise Gamgee, exemplifies unwavering friendship and undying loyalty.

Aragorn, the unwilling heir to the throne, takes a journey of self-discovery and rises as a noble and inspiring leader. The divided Gollum, once known as Sméagol, becomes a sad figure representing the toxic effect of the Ring on the mind. These complex images add to the emotional depth and relatability of the characters, transcending traditional fantasy stereotypes.

The Quest for the One Ring: A Journey of Peril and Redemption

The quest to destroy the One Ring is the story linchpin that pushes "The Lord of the Rings" into an epic journey. Frodo's journey from the Shire to Mount Doom is filled with dangers, challenges, and moral problems. The quest is not merely a physical trip but a deep study of character, morals, and the nature of power.

Frodo's mental fight against the evil impact of the Ring adds a psychic layer to the quest. The difficulties faced by the Fellowship—from the mines of Moria to the Battle of Helm's Deep—test their courage and friendship. The climactic moments at Mount Doom, where Frodo must make a fateful choice, embody the main themes of the story.

Linguistic Nuances: The Power of Words

Tolkien's linguistic brilliance goes beyond the creation of Elvish languages to the subtle use of language within the story. The writing on the Ring—"One

Ring to rule them all, One Ring to find them, One Ring to bring them all and in the darkness bind them"—captures the evil spirit of the Ring. The power of words is further demonstrated in prophesies, songs, and conversations that enrich the story weave.

Legacy and Contemporary Relevance: A Tale for the Ages

"The Lord of the Rings" has left an enduring mark on literature and popular culture, and its ideas and figures continue to echo in current conversations. The study of power, the complexities of friendship, and the moral aspects of suffering remain important in the face of current challenges. The narrative's lasting impact lies in its ability to inspire thought and prompt conversations on global themes that span the limits of time and genre.

Chapter 5: Professorship and Literary Impact

Academic Career at Oxford

Tolkien's Tenure as a Professor

J.R.R. Tolkien's academic work at the University of Oxford played a key role in shaping not only his personal and professional life but also the course of his writing projects. This chapter covers Tolkien's time as a professor, exploring his roles, inspirations, and the relationship between academics and creation.

Philology and Old English
    Tolkien's academic journey started with a deep interest in languages, particularly philology—the study of language in written history sources. His interest with linguistic development, Old English, and ancient writing set the basis for his later works, including the languages and myths of Middle-earth.

Tolkien's skill in Old English, combined with his creative approach to language creation, became a feature of his scholarly achievements. His praised lecture series on "Beowulf" and other Old English works displayed his ability to bridge the gap between study and storytelling, a skill that would prove important in the making of Middle-earth.

Appointment as Rawlinson and Bosworth Professor of Anglo-Saxon

In 1925, Tolkien took the post of Rawlinson and Bosworth Professor of Anglo-Saxon at Pembroke College, Oxford. This position not only signified a significant milestone in Tolkien's academic career but also provided him with a stage to dig deeper into his intellectual interests.

As a professor, Tolkien's interesting teaching style and love for his subject matter left a lasting effect on his pupils. His classes were known for their mix of language analysis, historical context, and a bit of storytelling—an approach that reflected the fusion of science and creativity visible in his creative works.

Lectures on Fantasy and Fairy Stories

Tolkien's academic efforts went beyond the limits of Old English writing. His famous talk, "On Fairy-Stories," given in 1939, studied the nature and purpose of fantasy writing. In this talk, Tolkien expressed his views on the inherent power of stories, the idea of the eucatastrophe (the sudden turn of events leading to a positive result), and the importance of sub-creation.

These ideas, given within an academic framework, offered insights into Tolkien's artistic philosophy and gave a theoretical basis for the imaginative world-building found in "The Hobbit" and "The Lord of the Rings." The talk stressed the deep influence of storytelling on human behavior and societal development.

Collegial Relationships and the Inklings

Tolkien's time at Oxford also allowed important relationships with fellow students, including C.S. Lewis, Charles Williams, and others who would form the informal literary discussion group known as the Inklings. The Inklings became a healthy ground for the exchange of ideas, reviews, and the sharing of artistic works.

The friendship within the Inklings played a key part in the growth of Tolkien's plots. The support and helpful comments he got from his peers added to the development of Middle-earth's lore and storytelling methods.

Balancing Academic and Creative Pursuits

Tolkien's ability to balance his academic duties with his artistic efforts showed his flexibility and commitment. While his academic work focused on philology and ancient literature, his evenings and weekends were often committed to the creation of languages, myths, and tales that would eventually become the basis of Middle-earth.

The smooth merging of his scholarly and artistic activities showed that, for Tolkien, the two were not mutually exclusive. Rather, they were interdependent, each improving and informing the other. His experiences as a philologist and medievalist deeply affected the language depth and historical validity of Middle-earth.

Influence on Future Generations of Writers

J.R.R. Tolkien's literary impact stretches far beyond his own lifetime, as his works have left an enduring mark on the world of fantasy literature. This chapter discusses the deep effect Tolkien has had on future generations of writers, exploring the ways in which his storytelling, world-building, and subject depth continue to shape the works of current authors.

Foundations of Modern Fantasy

Tolkien's influence on modern fantasy writing is important and changing. "The Hobbit" and "The Lord of the Rings" set a bar for grand writing, complex world-building, and the creation of engrossing secondary worlds. His works made the way for later generations of writers to explore the worlds of magic with a level of depth and complexity that was previously unparalleled.

Authors such as George R.R. Martin, J.K. Rowling, and countless others have acknowledged Tolkien's impact on their own artistic efforts. The classic hero's journey, the fight between light and darkness, and the creation of fully realized, internally consistent worlds—all features of Tolkien's writing—have become touchstones for writers looking to make compelling fantasy tales.

Linguistic Creativity and World-Building

Tolkien's skill in philology and linguistic creation has inspired writers to fill their works with rich, created languages and cultures. The Elvish languages, Dwarvish runes, and the linguistic variety of Middle-earth serve as a witness to Tolkien's commitment to linguistic accuracy. This linguistic creativity has influenced writers like Anthony Burgess, who created Nadsat in "A Clockwork Orange," and David J. Peterson, known for building languages for television shows like "Game of Thrones."

The careful attention to detail in Tolkien's world-building, from maps to histories, has set a standard for writers looking to create engaging and believable imaginary settings. Contemporary fantasy writers often draw inspiration from Tolkien's ability to build fully realized worlds that stretch beyond the immediate plot, encouraging readers to explore the depths of the imagined settings.

Exploration of Moral Complexity

Tolkien's study of moral complexity and the effects of power has connected with writers looking to fill their fantasy tales with depth and philosophical inquiry. The character of Gollum, the evil influence of the One Ring, and the complex depictions of heroes and baddies have encouraged writers to move beyond simple dichotomies and welcome shades of gray in their characterizations.

Writers like Ursula K. Le Guin, in her Earthsea series, and Philip Pullman, in the "His Dark Materials" trilogy, have drawn on Tolkien's model to build socially complicated and thought-provoking fantasy tales. The ethical problems faced by characters in Middle-earth have become a touchstone for exploring the details of good and evil in fantasy fiction.

Community and Literary Fellowship

Tolkien's experiences with the Inklings, a literary discussion group where writers shared and reviewed each other's works, have inspired modern writers to seek out and form similar communities. The value of cooperation, positive feedback, and the sharing of ideas within the writing community has become a legacy of Tolkien's approach to literary company.

Online writing communities, classes, and writing groups owe a debt to the friendship created by Tolkien and the Inklings. The realization that the creative process can be improved through shared experiences and different views has become a driving principle for writers in various fields.

Adaptations and Multimedia Influence

The great film versions of "The Lord of the Rings" by director Peter Jackson have further increased Tolkien's impact on the larger entertainment business. The tremendous success of these films has inspired writers to consider the potential of digital versions and the impact of visual stories on the acceptance of literary works.

Literary Impact and Popularity

The Rise of Tolkien Fandom

J.R.R. Tolkien's literary influence is not only obvious in the critical praise and academic acceptance of his works but also in the amazing rise of Tolkien fans. This chapter explores the far-reaching impact of Tolkien's works, the formation of committed fan groups, and the lasting fame that has made Middle-earth a cultural phenomenon.

Redefining Fantasy Literature

Tolkien's effect on the literary world is nothing short of revolutionary. "The Hobbit" and "The Lord of the Rings" not only changed the fantasy genre but also surpassed it, affecting the larger range of literature. The depth of Tolkien's world-building, the language wealth of his creations, and the thematic complexity of his tales raised fantasy from leisure to a genre capable of exploring deep truths and universal themes.

Writers across fields have acknowledged Tolkien's impact on their own works, noting the lasting memory of Middle-earth as a standard for imaginative stories. The effect stretches beyond writing, changing the way writers handle world-building, character development, and the study of moral and philosophical topics.

From Readers to Enthusiasts

The rise of Tolkien fans can be traced back to the passionate acceptance of his works by readers who, captivated by the wealth of Middle-earth, found ways to connect with like-minded admirers. As early as the 1960s, fan clubs and discussion groups dedicated to Tolkien's works began to form, creating places for fans to share their love for the stories, dig into the details of the tales, and discuss the deep themes buried in the narratives.

Tolkien Societies and Conventions

The creation of Tolkien clubs, such as The Tolkien Society and regional groups around the world, marked the formalization of Tolkien fans. These groups serve as places for fans to engage in academic talks, plan events, and enjoy the works of J.R.R. Tolkien. Annual meetings, like Oxonmoot and various regional events, provide opportunities for fans to come together, share their passion, and engage themselves in the lively culture of Middle-earth.

The impact of Tolkien fans is not limited to literature talks. It stretches to various kinds of artistic expression, including music, creative arts, and even live-action role-playing (LARPing). Fans often create original works inspired by Middle-earth, adding to a diverse and dynamic fan-generated lore.

From Books to Blockbusters

Tolkien's works, originally praised within literary groups, soon invaded popular culture, becoming a global phenomenon. The release of Peter Jackson's film versions of "The Lord of the Rings" in the early 2000s launched Tolkien into the popular consciousness. The pictures not only received critical praise but also presented Middle-earth to a new generation of fans.

The success of the film trilogy caused a rise in Tolkien-related products, video games, and extended media brands. The unique visual images of characters, settings, and famous scenes from the films became associated with Tolkien's legendarium, further strengthening its place in popular culture.

Online Fandom and Digital Communities

The rise of the internet aided the growth of Tolkien fans on a global scale. Online communities, social media groups, and fan websites became virtual meeting places for fans from various cultures and physical areas. The digital age has allowed fans to meet, share fan stories, participate in discussions, and collectively enjoy the lasting attraction of Middle-earth.

Digital platforms also provide places for fan-generated material, including podcasts, YouTube feeds, and blogs dedicated to studying every part of Tolkien's works. The online presence of Tolkien fans continues to change, ensuring that the excitement for Middle-earth stays lively and available to new generations of readers and watchers.

Cultural Impact and Adaptation

J.R.R. Tolkien's culture effect stretches far beyond the area of books, affecting art, music, language, and even changing the way viewers perceive and connect with magical worlds. This chapter discusses the deep cultural effect of Tolkien's works, from their adaptation into various media to the lasting influence on language and the arts.

Literature and Language

Tolkien's influence on writing is obvious, not only for the fantasy field but for stories as a whole. His careful world-building, complicated personalities, and thematic complexity have set a bar for ambitious writers. Many current writers, across genres, name Tolkien as a key inspiration, demonstrating the lasting impact of his story skill.

Moreover, Tolkien's creation of fully formed languages, such as Elvish and Dwarvish, has inspired scholars and language fans. The details of these created languages have become subjects of study and interest, showing how Tolkien's linguistic creativity has transcended the pages of his books.

Film Adaptations: Bringing Middle-earth to the Screen

The film versions of "The Lord of the Rings" and "The Hobbit" by director Peter Jackson marked a movie milestone and presented Tolkien's legendarium to a global audience. The success of these films not only won critical praise but also affected the world of filmmaking, especially in the fantasy field.

The visual wealth of Middle-earth, as presented in the films, has become the ultimate image for many fans. The success of the versions has spurred further interest in adapting fantasy books for the screen, adding to a film rebirth of epic storytelling.

Television and Streaming: Expanding Middle-earth

With the rise of streaming services, new versions of Tolkien's works have appeared, offering to explore unknown areas within Middle-earth. These projects, whether based on known material or unique tales inspired by Tolkien's world, continue to add to the cultural conversation around Middle-earth.

Television shows, such as "The Lord of the Rings: The Rings of Power," aim to dig deeper into the lore and give a new take on known stories. The reworking of Tolkien's works into episodic forms shows the lasting appetite for tales set in the vast and highly detailed world he built.

Visual Arts: Inspiring Creativity

Tolkien's effect is widespread in the visual arts, inspiring generations of artists to interpret and rethink his figures and settings. Illustrations, paintings, and digital art capture the spirit of Middle-earth in varied styles, giving viewers with new views on familiar scenes.

The visual expression of Tolkien's works stretches to book covers, products, and different kinds of fan art. The unique style of Middle-earth, shaped by both Tolkien's writings and the visual versions of artists, has become an important part of the cultural image connected with fantasy fiction.

Music and Soundtracks: A Sonic Journey

The musical dimension of Tolkien's works is apparent not only in versions but also in the creation of original compositions inspired by Middle-earth. Scores written for film versions, such as Howard Shore's work on "The Lord of the Rings," have become famous and associated with the epic nature of Tolkien's tales.

Beyond film tunes, numerous bands and artists across styles have taken inspiration from Tolkien's works. The themes of courage, loss, and the fight between light and evil echo through vocal works, adding to the cultural tapestry connected with Middle-earth.

Gaming and Interactive Media: Immersive Experiences

Tolkien's influence stretches to the world of games, where interactive versions and original works set in Middle-earth offer players engaging experiences. Video games, role-playing games, and internet platforms allow viewers to explore the environments, meet people, and join in their own tales within the vast world of Tolkien's creation.

The interactive nature of games allows fans to connect with Tolkien's legendarium in unique ways, adding to a dynamic and developing relationship between books and interactive media.

Chapter 6: Personal Life and Relationships

Marriage and Family

Tolkien's Love Story with Edith Bratt

J.R.R. Tolkien's personal life, marked by a deep love story with Edith Bratt, is an important part of his storyline. This chapter discusses the marriage between Tolkien and Edith, their lasting partnership, and the family bonds that shaped Tolkien's life and affected his artistic efforts.

Early Encounters: The Blossoming Connection
Tolkien's friendship with Edith Bratt began during their school years in Birmingham, England. Both children, they found comfort and friendship in each other's company. Their bond strengthened through shared hobbies, including a desire for books, languages, and a love for nature—a theme that would later echo heavily in Tolkien's works.

However, the initial years of their relationship faced resistance from Tolkien's guardian, Father Francis Morgan, who disapproved of the romance. This task only increased the couple's determination and added a layer of defiance to their love story.

Separation and Reunion: A Test of Devotion
Tolkien and Edith's link faced a major hurdle when Tolkien joined in the

army during World War I. The split tried the strength of their bond, but the exchange of letters between the couple during this time showed the depth of their love and commitment.

Upon Tolkien's return from the war, their meeting marked a turning point in their relationship. The difficulties they faced only strengthened their dedication to each other, and Tolkien commonly referred to this period as a "dark time" that eventually led to a better future.

The Marriage of Beren and Lúthien

Tolkien's own love story with Edith served as a deep inspiration for one of the most famous romances within his legendarium—the tale of Beren and Lúthien. The similarities between the fictional couple and Tolkien's own experiences are obvious, with both tales exploring themes of love, sacrifice, and the victory of devotion over hardship.

The gravestone shared by J.R.R. and Edith Tolkien bears the words "Beren" and "Lúthien," a touching acknowledgment of the deep effect their love story had on Tolkien's artistic work.

Family Life: Joy and Challenges

The marriage of J.R.R. and Edith Tolkien bloomed into a family life marked by joy, creativity, and the difficulties of balancing personal and professional interests. The couple had four children: John, Michael, Christopher, and Priscilla. The duties of parenting and the pressures of Tolkien's academic work produced a lively home, where stories became a beloved family ritual.

Tolkien's devotion to his family, coupled with Edith's support, influenced the creation of narratives that resonated with themes of familial bonds, friendship, and the enduring power of love—a theme not only explored in "The Lord of the Rings" but also in lesser-known works such as "Smith of Wootton Major."

Legacy of Love: The Influence on Middle-earth

The love between J.R.R. Tolkien and Edith Bratt left a lasting mark on Middle-earth. The theme of love, often tried by hardship and separation, is woven into the fabric of Tolkien's tales. From the heartbreaking tale of Aragorn and Arwen to the lasting friendship of Frodo and Sam, the impact of Tolkien's personal experiences with love and family is obvious in the emotional depth of his characters and their relationships.

The creation of the Evenstar pendant as a gift from Aragorn to Arwen, reflecting a similar real-life gift from Tolkien to Edith, is a beautiful example of how their personal experiences found expression within the magical world of Middle-earth.

The Joys and Challenges of Family Life

J.R.R. Tolkien's family life, marked by the joys and difficulties of having four children alongside a busy writing career, offers a glimpse into the complex fabric of his personal experiences. This chapter discusses the family relationships, the times of joy, and the inevitable difficulties that shaped Tolkien's role as a husband and father.

Creating a Family: The Arrival of John, Michael, Christopher, and Priscilla
The Tolkien family started with the marriage of J.R.R. and Edith, a union that bloomed into a home filled with the laughter and energy of four children. John, the eldest, was born in 1917, followed by Michael in 1920, Christopher in 1924, and Priscilla in 1929. The presence of children brought an extra layer of kindness and liveliness to the Tolkien home.

The Influence of Parenthood on Tolkien's Work
Parenthood played a major part in Tolkien's artistic activities. Bedtime stories and tales spun for his children often became the seeds of plots that would later find their way into Middle-earth. Tolkien's tale sessions became beloved family routines, fostering a love for plots and creativity among his

children.

The bedtime tales of Roverandom and Mr. Bliss, stories made to entertain his children, demonstrate Tolkien's ability to make interesting storylines for a young audience.

Balancing Academia and Family

Tolkien's loyalty to his academic work offered difficulties in balancing business duties with family life. As a philologist and professor, Tolkien faced the pressures of teaching, study, and managerial tasks. Navigating the delicate balance between school and family took careful time management and a committed effort to be present for his wife and children.

The Influences of War

The start of World War II brought a new set of problems to the Tolkien family. The split caused by Tolkien's service in the Home Guard and the sharing of resources tried the strength of family ties. The letters shared during this period, especially between Tolkien and his son Christopher, provide touching insights into the difficulties faced by families during times of war.

Joyful Moments

Amidst the challenges, the Tolkien family built ongoing customs and honored times of joy. Holidays, birthdays, and special events became chances for shared fun and the making of memorable memories. The Christmas letters from Father Christmas, a custom Tolkien kept for his children, demonstrate the imaginative and festive spirit that filled the Tolkien home.

Familial Bonds in Middle-eart

The themes of family, friendship, and loyalty that echo throughout Tolkien's works are reflective of his own experiences. The bonds between Frodo and Sam, the friendship among the Fellowship, and the familial ties within the Hobbit society mirror the valued relationships within the Tolkien family. The complexity of these interactions adds depth and believability to the people filling Middle-earth.

Navigating Loss: Coping with the Passing of Edith

The passing of Edith in 1971 marked a deep loss for Tolkien. The lasting bond they shared throughout their marriage was a source of strength and inspiration. Navigating life as a widower offered its own set of challenges, yet Tolkien's love for his family and the memory of the events they shared continued to shape his later years.

Friendship and Fellowship

The Inklings and Tolkien's Literary Friendships

J.R.R. Tolkien's life was improved by deep bonds that stretched beyond casual company to become a source of inspiration and intellectual bonding. This chapter discusses the importance of friendship in Tolkien's life, especially his connection with the Inklings, a literary group that played a key role in forming his creative efforts.

The Inklings: A Literary Brotherhood

The Inklings, a literary study group started in the 1930s, became a laboratory for the sharing of ideas and artistic discovery. Comprising famous people such as C.S. Lewis, Charles Williams, Owen Barfield, and others, the Inklings gave Tolkien with a helpful and mentally stimulating setting.

The group met weekly to talk their works-in-progress, share readings, and participate in heated discussions. The lively exchanges within the Inklings drove Tolkien's creative process, giving helpful feedback and creating an atmosphere of mutual support.

C.S. Lewis: A Kindred Spirit and Collaborator

Among the Inklings, the friendship between J.R.R. Tolkien and C.S. Lewis stands out as one of the most lasting and important. Bonding over their shared love for myth, language, and stories, the two writers formed a similar spirit that stretched beyond the literary realm.

The friendship with Lewis went beyond idle talks; it was a deep partnership. The two writers shared copies of their works, gave critical comments, and affected each other's artistic decisions. Lewis, in particular, played a key role in pushing Tolkien to finish and print "The Lord of the Rings."

Friendship as a Theme in Middle-earth

The idea of friendship is carefully sewn into the fabric of Middle-earth. The Fellowship of the Ring, featuring figures like Frodo, Sam, Aragorn, Gandalf, and others, demonstrates the power and depth of friendship. The challenges faced by the Fellowship mirror the trials and successes of real-life bonds, stressing the value of loyalty, trust, and shared purpose.

The camaraderie among the members of the Fellowship, especially the lasting bond between Frodo and Sam, shows the deep effect of friendship on Tolkien's writing. These relationships add emotional depth to the story, making Middle-earth a place where the power of friendship plays a key part in beating hardship.

Intellectual Exchange

The Inklings' intellectual conversation left a lasting mark on Tolkien's creative works. The talks and debates within the group impacted the growth of Middle-earth, adding to the depth of its languages, cultures, and myths.

The support and helpful feedback got from fellow Inklings helped improve Tolkien's ideas and tales. The shared dedication to quality and a deep respect for each other's work produced an environment where imagination thrived, allowing Tolkien to bring to fruition the complex world he had envisioned.

Legacy of Friendship: Beyond the Inklings

The effect of friendship went beyond the Inklings to other important people in Tolkien's life. His ties with people like George Sayer, a former student and historian, and Christopher Wiseman, a close friend and fellow researcher, offered additional layers of support and intellectual exchange.

The bonds formed within and outside the Inklings became a testament to the lasting nature of similar souls. These ties, marked by mutual respect and shared love for books, added depth to Tolkien's life and impact.

Influences of Close Relationships on Tolkien's Works

J.R.R. Tolkien's literary works were not only shaped by his lively mind but also deeply affected by the close relationships and personal experiences that marked his life. This chapter dives into the complex web of links, feelings, and the effect of important relationships on the creation of Middle-earth.

Marriage and Love: Edith Bratt as Lúthien

The love between J.R.R. Tolkien and Edith Bratt served as a basic impact on Tolkien's works. The couple's deep bond, lasting through the trials of war and the tests of time, found expression in the moving tale of Beren and Lúthien in Middle-earth.

Edith, whom Tolkien often referred to as his Lúthien, inspired the figure of the Elven princess in "The Silmarillion." The story matches the couple's own experiences, showing themes of love, suffering, and the quest of lasting beauty that echoed throughout their lives.

Friendship and Fellowship

Real-Life Companions in Middle-earth

The deep bonds developed in Tolkien's life left a lasting mark on his creative works. The friendship among the Inklings, especially with C.S. Lewis, seeped into the tales of Middle-earth. The lasting ties of the Fellowship of the Ring, the loyal friendship between Frodo and Sam, and the shared journey of characters reflected the strength of real-life friendships.

The intellectual discussion, arguments, and praise within the Inklings gave Tolkien with the support needed to bring his complex world to life. The effect of similar spirits on the making of Middle-earth was an important part of Tolkien's creative process.

Fatherhood: Family Bonds in Middle-earth

Tolkien's experiences as a father improved his picture of family ties in Middle-earth. The joys and difficulties of having four children found echoes in the tales. The bedtime tales given to his children, the creation of amusing figures like Roverandom, and the inclusion of family rituals all added to the domestic kindness evident in his works.

The ideas of parenthood, suffering, and the lasting power of family ties are woven into the fabric of Middle-earth. The love shared among figures like Aragorn and Arwen, as well as the family ties within the Hobbit community, show the emotional depth drawn from Tolkien's own role as a father.

Loss and Grief

The experience of loss, particularly the passing of Edith, affected Tolkien's picture of sadness in Middle-earth. Characters like Frodo, who bears the load of the One Ring and feels the weight of the world, echo the author's own battles with loss and the changing scenery of life.

Tolkien's exploration of death, immortality, and the bittersweet nature of existence in Middle-earth reflects his study of deep themes that came from personal experiences of joy, love, and, eventually, loss.

Chapter 7: Later Years and Legacy

Posthumous Publications

The Silmarillion and Beyond

J.R.R. Tolkien's literary impact goes beyond his lifetime, with later releases showing a treasure trove of unfinished works, notes, and tales. This chapter explores the journey of bringing Tolkien's unfinished writings to readers, focused on "The Silmarillion" and other works that came after the author's passing.

Tolkien's Unpublished Works

At the time of J.R.R. Tolkien's death in 1973, he left behind a vast collection of unfinished writings, notes, and drafts that gave looks into the huge world of Middle-earth. Among these materials, "The Silmarillion" stood as a core piece, a gathering of mythopoeic tales and basic narratives that laid the base for Tolkien's wider legendarium.

Christopher Tolkien's Editorial Role

Christopher Tolkien, J.R.R. Tolkien's son, played a key part in organizing and reviewing his father's secret writings. As the literary agent of the Tolkien estate, Christopher began the difficult task of sorting the vast material into logical tales. His editing efforts put life into his father's unwritten tales, providing readers with a better understanding of the complex history that underpins Middle-earth.

The Silmarillion: A Mythopoeic Masterpiece

Published in 1977, "The Silmarillion" exposed readers to the fictional past and basic stories of Middle-earth. The work, edited and collected by Christopher Tolkien, dives into the creation of the world, the battles between the Valar and Melkor, and the fates of Elves, Men, and Dwarves. The patchwork of "The Silmarillion" improves the reader's understanding of the events leading up to "The Hobbit" and "The Lord of the Rings."

Unfinished Tales and The History of Middle-earth Series

Beyond "The Silmarillion," Christopher Tolkien continued to reveal his father's work through different publications. "Unfinished Tales" (1980) offered a collection of unfinished tales and articles, giving extra views into the people and events of Middle-earth.

The massive "History of Middle-earth" series, covering twelve books and released between 1983 and 1996, looks into the development of Tolkien's works. The series includes early works, language studies, and different versions of well-known stories, giving fans a complete view of the author's creative process.

The Children of Húrin and Beren and Lúthien

In the 21st century, Christopher Tolkien released solo works that further built upon specific tales from "The Silmarillion." "The Children of Húrin" (2007) and "Beren and Lúthien" (2017) gave thorough studies of these tales, showing them in a unified and understandable manner.

These books offered readers a chance to immerse themselves in the sad fate of the Children of Húrin and the lasting love story of Beren and Lúthien, both vital components of the wider legendarium.

The Role of Christopher Tolkien in Preserving His Father's Legacy

The memory of J.R.R. Tolkien, the creator of Middle-earth, owes much of its protection and growth to the committed efforts of his son, Christopher Tolkien. This chapter discusses the complex role Christopher played in protecting, organizing, and sharing his father's vast body of work, ensuring that the enchanting world of Middle-earth continued to fascinate audiences worldwide.

The Literary Executor: Christopher Tolkien's Stewardship

Following J.R.R. Tolkien's passing in 1973, Christopher took the vital job of literary manager for the Tolkien estate. This duty tasked him with managing his father's secret writings, notes, and drafts, a responsibility that needed both a deep understanding of his father's vision and a commitment to keeping the purity of Middle-earth.

Editing "The Silmarillion": A Herculean Task

One of Christopher's most massive tasks was editing and collecting "The Silmarillion," a work left unfinished at the time of J.R.R. Tolkien's death. Christopher looked through an extensive array of works, putting together the magical tales that formed the basis of Middle-earth. His editing skill and commitment to truth guaranteed that "The Silmarillion" not only honors his father's purpose but also stood as a literary masterpiece in its own right.

Curator of Unfinished Tales and The History of Middle-earth

In addition to "The Silmarillion," Christopher started on the big project of releasing "Unfinished Tales" (1980). This compilation featured unfinished tales and studies into the history of Middle-earth, giving readers with a better understanding of the characters and events.

The "History of Middle-earth" series, containing twelve books released between 1983 and 1996, highlighted Christopher's careful editing of his father's developing works. This thorough series showed the complex layers of J.R.R. Tolkien's creative process, giving students and fans rare access to the growth of Middle-earth.

Standalone Works: The Children of Húrin and Beren and Lúthien

Christopher Tolkien's devotion to his father's legacy stretched to the release of separate works that built upon specific tales from "The Silmarillion." "The Children of Húrin" (2007) and "Beren and Lúthien" (2017) were organized and presented by Christopher, giving readers with in-depth studies of these tales in forms available to a bigger audience.

Preserving Artistic Vision and Linguistic Expertise

Beyond his editing role, Christopher Tolkien protected his father's artistic vision and language skill. His commitment to keeping the languages created by J.R.R. Tolkien, such as Elvish and Dwarvish speech, added to the realism and engaging quality of Middle-earth.

A Legacy Beyond Editing: Lectures and Advocacy

Christopher Tolkien's efforts went beyond the world of writing. He participated in talks and interviews, sharing insights into his father's work and the process of bringing Middle-earth to life. Additionally, he was a champion for the protection of J.R.R. Tolkien's legacy, heavily involved in court fights to defend the purity of his father's works.

Legacy in Popular Culture

Tolkien's Enduring Impact on Literature, Film, and Art

J.R.R. Tolkien's impact stretches far beyond the pages of his books, influencing various parts of popular culture. This chapter dives into the lasting impact of Tolkien's imagination, studying how his works have left a permanent mark on literature, film, and art, changing the cultural landscape for decades.

Shaping Fantasy and Beyond

J.R.R. Tolkien's influence on writing, especially within the fantasy field, is immeasurable. His complex world-building, languages, and subtle personalities set a bar for later generations of writers. Authors such as George R.R. Martin, J.K. Rowling, and countless others recognize Tolkien's impact in creating the world of modern fantasy writing.

The creation of new sub-genres, such as high fantasy, owes much to Tolkien's innovative approach to writing. His focus on building fully realized imaginary worlds with rich histories and languages has become a feature of fantasy writing.

Film Adaptations: Bringing Middle-earth to Life

The film versions of J.R.R. Tolkien's works have presented Middle-earth to a global audience in an artistically stunning way. Director Peter Jackson's film trilogies, "The Lord of the Rings" (2001-2003) and "The Hobbit" (2012-2014), not only earned critical praise but also became popular icons.

These versions displayed the promise of fantasy stories on the big screen, utilizing cutting-edge technology to bring to life Tolkien's epic settings, famous characters, and exciting fights. The success of these films opened the way for other fantasy series and cemented Tolkien's place in film history.

Artistic Influence: Inspiring Illustrators and Visual Artists

Tolkien's colorful descriptions and detailed tales have inspired a multitude of designers and visual artists. The unique visual style of artists like Alan Lee and John Howe, who worked with Tolkien on different projects and added to the film versions, has become linked with Middle-earth.

Beyond drawing, Tolkien's works have inspired a wide number of artistic forms, from paintings and statues to digital art and graphic design. The wealth of Middle-earth's visual weave continues to captivate artists who seek to capture the spirit of Tolkien's works.

Cultural Impact: Language, Music, and Beyond

Tolkien's influence stretches beyond writing and visual arts into the worlds of language and music. Linguists study Tolkien's created languages, such as Elvish and Dwarvish, as examples of complex language creation. Additionally, different musical works inspired by Middle-earth, including Howard Shore's famous film themes, have added to the cultural impact of Tolkien's world.

Tolkien's impact on gaming culture is obvious in the success of fantasy role-playing games and video games set in places reminiscent of Middle-earth. Games like Dungeons & Dragons draw inspiration from Tolkien's mythopoeic stories, showing the lasting impact of his imaginative contributions.

Fan Communities: A Global Fellowship

Tolkien's work has fostered a lively and global group of fans. Conventions, fan groups, and internet sites provide places for followers to enjoy their shared love for Middle-earth. The enthusiasm of these fans has led to a continued study and growth of Tolkien's world through fan literature, art, and scholarly talks.

Celebration of Tolkien in Fan Communities

J.R.R. Tolkien's literary works have sparked a global company of fans who come together to enjoy and immerse themselves in the enchanting world of Middle-earth. This chapter discusses the lively and diverse fan groups that have developed, showing the ways in which enthusiasts share their love for Tolkien's works.

Conventions and Gatherings: Fellowship Beyond Pages

Fan events dedicated to J.R.R. Tolkien provide places for fans to come together and revel in their shared passion. Events like Tolkien Moot, Oxonmoot, and Dragon Con's Tolkien Track offer stages for fans to discuss their favorite books, share artistic works, and participate in lively discussions about the details of Middle-earth.

These meetings go beyond standard traditions; they represent a sense of unity that matches the friendship found among characters in Tolkien's tales. Fans often dress as their favorite characters, join in panel talks, and engage in engaging activities that bring Middle-earth to life.

Online Forums and Communities: Digital Realms of Middle-earth

The digital age has given rise to vast online groups and communities where Tolkien fans from around the world can meet. Platforms like TheOneRing.net, Reddit's r/tolkienfans, and different Discord groups provide places for conversations, fan ideas, and the sharing of fan-created material.

These online groups serve as virtual meeting places for fans who may be geographically separated but share a shared love for Middle-earth. Discussions range from serious studies of Tolkien's languages to fan stories and artwork inspired by the rich fabric of his works.

Fan Fiction and Art

Tolkien's vast and detailed world offers rich ground for fan creation. Fan fiction writers dig into hidden tales, exploring characters and plotlines beyond the scope of the original works. From epics set in the Second Age to character-centric short stories, fan fiction puts new life into Middle-earth.

Artists within the fan group add to the visual complexity of Tolkien's world. Illustrations, digital art, and even handmade things like maps and jewelry pay respect to the scenery, animals, and people of Middle-earth. Social media platforms like Instagram, DeviantArt, and Tumblr serve as sites where fans display their artistic versions.

Role-Playing and Gaming: Interactive Middle-earth Adventures

Role-playing games, both board and digital, provide fans with realistic experiences in Tolkien's world. Games like Middle-earth: Shadow of Mordor,

The Lord of the Rings Online, and board RPGs like Adventures in Middle-earth allow players to step into the shoes of people traveling the environments of Middle-earth.

These engaging experiences offer fans a unique chance to explore the lore, meet familiar places and characters, and even create their own tales within the rich framework given by Tolkien's works.

Tolkien Reading Day: An Annual Celebration

Established by The Tolkien Society, Tolkien Reading Day is a yearly event observed on March 25th, the date of the defeat of Sauron in "The Lord of the Rings." Fans worldwide participate by reading and sharing their favorite passages from Tolkien's works, fostering a sense of global unity in celebrating the author's contributions to literature.

Printed in Dunstable, United Kingdom

67923036R00037